CAR RENTAL BUSINESS

WITH JUST ONE CAR

Lessons from the trenches and learning the hard way ...by doing things that didn't work. Doing things that worked mildly well and Doing things that worked widly "well"

STEP BY STEP GUIDE FOR SUCCESSESSFUL ENTREPRENEURS

Ignatius Gwabada

(spine) START YOUR OWN CAR RENTAL BUSINESS WITH JUST ONE CAR

Published in South Africa

Gwabada, Ignatius.

Start Your Own Car Rental Business with Just One Car/by Ignatius Gwabada

ISBN-13: 978-1500548278

Printed in South Africa

Table of Contents

**As part of this book I have included some free bonus Car Rental Business templates that you can start using right away. These templates are in word so that you can edit them to your liking and add your company name and logo. To get access visit and register on www.startyourowncarrental.co.za. **

1. Introduction/Disclaimer

I don't believe in "get rich quick," but I do believe it's entirely possible to "get rich" if you work hard, provide a lot of value to your customers, and are not afraid to ask for money in return for the value you provide. The important information and resources in this book will help you create a Car Rental Business that generates an extra income for you if you are a beginner and wealth for your family if you grow the business.

I make no guarantees about your ability to get results or earn any money with the ideas, strategies, and tactics described in this book. My goal is to highlight how I did it and how I helped other start-ups like you, provide you with the steps I followed, and show you the road map you can follow. Each reader will pick up this book with different experiences and skills. Whether you succeed or not depends on how well you persist through adversity and how you acquire the skills you don't have.

This book contains step by step How to Guides, all the car rental business documents you need to get started such as Checklists, Car Rental contracts and a decade of dedicated study of what works in the car rental business. Although I believe the content is accurate, complete, and current, I make no warranty as to its accuracy, completeness, or currency. It is your responsibility to verify any information before relying on it.

Don't construe anything in this book as legal advice. I'm not an attorney, and I'm not practicing law. If you need legal advice, please seek the advice of legal counsel. I hope the "lessons learned" and steps outlined in this guideline book will help you launch a successful Car Rental Business generating quick, sustainable wealth for you and your family.

2. The Car Rental Business Model That Generates Sustainable Wealth

"When we are sure that we are on the right road there is no need to plan our journey too far ahead. No need to burden ourselves with doubts and fears as to the obstacles that may bar our progress. We cannot take more than one step at a time."
Orison Swett Marden

Some men seem to attract success, wealth, attainment, power, with very little conscious effort; others conquer with great difficulty; still others fail altogether to reach their ambitions, desires and ideals. Some people get rich while others toil for decades and die with nothing to show for it. Other business models allow their owners to work normal workweeks, take vacations, and generate millions of dollars in "take-out-of the-business" profits that give them the freedom all business owners dream about. There are profound differences in the types of businesses that generate quick, sustainable wealth for their owners. You won't become successful or wealthy without work, but success is not a result of working harder than everyone else. It's about building a business with specific attributes that enable you to accumulate wealth.

People all around you are getting rich. Why are they getting rich? Because they are doing things that generate more money than they spend, allowing them to accumulate wealth. They have the money "Blueprint" It all boils down to behaviour.

You aren't holding one of those self-help books that tell you what you imagine will come true. This is the book that gives you the road map of how you can make your dreams come true starting and running a Car Rental Business that generates more money than you spend.

If you follow the step-by-step paths outlined within these pages, you will build a life that surpasses what you can imagine today. In the next few pages, I'll reveal the dependable Car Rental Business model.

Within this book you'll read examples of what works, what doesn't work, mistakes to avoid, examples of actual marketing material I used and the actual business documents that you will need in order to hit the ground running.

Five simple criteria will help you determine if a business has the power to generate wealth or if it will merely dominate your time and provide you with few results. Before you launch a new business, you need to ask yourself these questions:

- **Is it a Proven Business model**? Has the business been proven to generate wealth for others in the past? For instance, if you don't see anyone getting rich as a teacher, driver or by being a technician, it's a good guess that you won't get wealthy that way either. Instead, look for a consistent pattern of a good percentage of business owners getting rich within the industry; technology, real estate, and car rental are proven winners from the past. Wealth isn't produced by thinking, dreaming, or imagining what you want. Money doesn't care what you think about most. Money is attracted to you when you create a business that produces value for paying customers.

- **Does it have a large business scope?** How big can it get, can you push volumes, and can you go from one market place to another.

- **Are there high margins?** Selling products at higher prices with a low production cost allows you to do much more marketing. Instead, get into businesses with high margins to make it easier for you to generate a healthy profit.

- **Is there a low start-up investment?** Too many business owners invest their entire life savings into a venture only to discover there is no market for their new products. Instead, keep your investments low. This way, even if you make a mistake, it won't be financially devastating to you. Plus, it will allow you to start multiple businesses over time to generate more wealth as your skills improve.

- **Is there risk:** Of course there is risk just like any entrepreneur, you have to be a bit of a risk taker. Any adventure whether it's in your business life or personal life, there is always inherent risk, however the key thing is learning how other entrepreneurs did it and what methods worked, what didn't work, mistakes they made and how they came out rich on the other side.

I stumbled upon the car rental business myself about a decade ago out of necessity. I worked for a large I.T. company in Johannesburg. Since I was a contractor my contract expired and was never renewed because the company was experiencing financial difficulty. I found myself with no job; endless debts left right and centre. At the same time I had a family to feed, rent to pay. All I had was just one car, a Nissan Almera, fortunately enough

I had finished paying for this car so it no longer belonged to the bank.

My landlord evicted me and my family from a 2 bed apartment we were renting. In order to make ends meet I moved my wife and kids to go stay with my brother. I found myself sleeping in the car and bathing in public toilets. I started by operating a taxi business, all I used to do was park my car outside night clubs and carry drunk people for a fee. Things were not that rosy because in the taxi business you need a licence to operate, I didn't have that. Thus I used to carry a removable taxi sign in my car; I would only display it when the car was parked outside night clubs and remove it once on the road to avoid attracting cops.

Things started getting better but I discovered that I was trading hours for dollars. I was producing value, but not within a business model that charged a fair price for the value it provided its customers. I began studying these Car Rental operators. They had created a business model with high margins, flexibility for its owner as well as stability.

I quickly changed the model from taxi business to Car Rental starting with just one car. For the last ten years, I've used tried and tested different car rental business strategies to build many car rental businesses in different countries, all with fewer than two full-time employees. These businesses are as lucrative as they are easy to operate, but when I explain the business model, it's easy for the inexperienced or the cynical to dismiss it. You may recognise a component or two, but it's how the components work together that gives the Car Rental Business power.

This book isn't just for reading. Think of it as an owner's manual for the most lucrative business in the world. You'll learn how to build it and run it for success and profit. While most of this book focuses on how you create and run your own Car Rental business, let me first explain why this business surpasses all others in opportunity, sustainability, and profit.

Advantages of a Car Rental Business:

1. You can start making money right away. Large profit potential exists.
2. If you are someone who loves meeting new people, this is your business.
3. You can easily grow in less than a year.

4. There is always demand for car rentals.

5. You can sell cars to your car rental customers, especially loyal customers that always pay on time.

6. Few staff members are necessary.

7. Little investment is needed to get started. You can start with just one car.

Just like any business there are risks involved, however the risks of this business are quite few and are outweighed by the benefits. Below is a list of some of the risks:

1. Car theft is rife; you need the right protective measures in place to protect your investment.

2. Bad clients, refusing to pay.

3. Fraud by clients.

4. Depreciation of cars.

1.1. Dissecting The Car Rental Business Model

The Car Rental Business operating model comprises of the following things: **People, Process, Directives and Technology.**

Find below the Business Operating Model

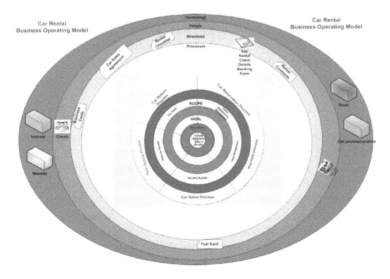

The key components in a Car Rental Business Model that generate Quick, Sustainable Wealth are People, Process, Technology and Directives. The Technology component comprises of Email, Telephone, and Website which is a sub component of the internet. The People component is the business owner and the clients. Directives refer to the business forms such as car rental contracts, rental checklists, which are the documents that give instructions or are prescriptive as to how the business should be run. The inner circles refer to processes involved in the Car Rental Business such as Car Reservation process, payment process, fleet service process and car sales process. The target or objective is to provide affordable cars to clients.

The car rental business operates based on the following three models:

1.2.   Daily & Monthly rentals

A car rental basically is a vehicle that can be used temporarily for a fee. In most cases people rent out cars when they go for a vacation, business trips, change location, have been involved in an accident or their car is being serviced. These types of clients form the bulk of Daily car rental business because they need the car for a short period of time, in most cases less than seven days. Why? They need a car because of convenience. Getting a car rental assists those who need to get around despite the fact they do not have access to their own personal vehicle or they don't even own a car at all. Then there are clients who might need a car for at least a month, these clients are people who are waiting to buy they own car or they can't get car financing for various reasons. Exhibits 7 & 8 show two types of rental contracts, that is the Daily Rental agreement and the Long term rental contract. Preferably you would want your clients to rent cars for a very long time thus having predictable cash flow in the business, especially if you are just starting.

1.3.   Rent to buy

Rent to buy model works in such a way that you buy cars and lease them out to clients in such a way that at the end of the lease the client owns the car. This is a good model if you want a hustle free business. In this model a Rent To Buy agreement is signed between the owner and lessee, this agreement can be anything form six months to twenty four months depending on the agreement. Exhibit 9 shows a sample of the Rent to Buy Agreement. Keys things to consider in this model are that insurance and car maintenance must come at the client's expense. In what cases do you go for this model? It's suitable in cases where you don't want hands on approach to the business and in situations where you need to get rid of high maintenance cars on your fleet.

1.4. Car Sales

The moment you start a car rental business you will be automatically involved in the car sales business. The reason I say so is that at some moment when you rent out cars you will need to dispose of old cars, and how do you do that? You sell them. Thus it's important to understand how to maximise profits by selling cars at the right time before they become liabilities rather than cash cows.

Take Away

Find a good name for your car rental business; people like to hire cars from companies rather than individuals.

3.　Set your Goals

"Anyone who has never made a mistake has never tried something new."

Albert Einstein

Don't get started until you have SMART goals; Specific, Measurable, Achievable, Relevant and Time based goals. Here is how to use this tool to go beyond fuzzy goals into building a successful car rental business.

Specific
Obtain five cars by the end of the year. This goal is well defined and favourable. Remember to start small. One step at a time.

Measurable
This business is a game of numbers. You have to measure to the last cent otherwise you might think that you are making money whilst you are not.
Put down concrete numbers such as:
1) Cost of traffic fines
2) Cost used per car on toll roads
3) Car disc renewal cost
4) Service cost. Keep track of all service intervals for each car and when it will need to get serviced
5) Keep track of when each car licence disc is due for renewal

Achievable
This book is a guideline on how to start a successful car rental business with no assistance from the banks.
Once you set your target goals, there are three things you need to develop:

1. Power and ability
2. Capacity: Can you provide enough cars to service your clients as in when required?
3. Knowledge: Do you have the knowledge of good client service and how to deliver first class customer service?

Relevant
In this world of technological change staying relevant is the key to survive.
Keep your car rental business relevant in your location. A good example is that when new train station is established, how you are going to keep your business alive and better. Continuous research and innovation is key to staying in the business.

Time

Your business goals and objectives must be marked with specific time frames. The time to start is now. In this business clients call in anytime of the day looking for cars. There is no 8h00 – 17h00 mentality. This is a 24/7 365 days a year business and if you can't work these hours then this business is not for you.

4.   Screw the Banks & Santa Claus

"Nobody can give you freedom. Nobody can give you equality or justice
or anything. If you are a man you take it"
Malcolm X

When I first started the car rental business I approached all the banks
everywhere with my business plan and financial statements looking for
capital to grow the business. Guess what? Nobody gave me a cent. I
even approached friends or would be investors and showed them the
numbers, the long term plan. Guess what, none of them gave me
money. You might be in the same boat as I was but don't despair. Here
is my experience of Santa.

"I was raised by a single mother; we used to stay in a one room house,
with a single paraffin stove and I would sleep on the floor with just one
blanket. During Christmas time my mother used to send me to my
relatives' house that happen to stay in Borrowdale which is a low density
surburb.Each year my cousin Tendai used to ask Santa for new things
such as a bicycle and he would get it. I really wanted a bicycle as well so
I would ask Santa for a bicycle year after year but never got it. My
cousin Tendai would have new clothes and my mother would buy me
second hand clothes. So the cycle continued every year, I would ask
Santa for whatever my cousins (in a much better off family) asked for.

One year a bicycle; they got a bicycle; and I got second hand clothes.

Every year, thinking I was making a mistake in my letters to Santa, I
carefully copied my cousin's letter to Santa word for word, asking politely
for a bicycle. My cousins got bikes; I got second hand clothes.

One day I decided that I had had enough of Santa, so I set about being
my own Santa Claus for the rest of my life.

Hopefully the points are obvious: most people childishly rely on others to
give, to appoint, to authorise, to promote, to grant permission, to set
their life agendas for them, to give them jobs, to give them money to
start businesses.

Only a comparative few accept full and total responsibility to be their
own Santa and grant their own requests. Take matters into your own
hands and start something that will create wealth for you and your
family.

14

There isn't any fat guy in a red suit coming down your chimney to bring you that Mercedes Benz you're lusting after or that fat retirement account that'll guarantee your security. Forget it my friend. Screw Santa and the Banks.

Take Away

Be your own Santa

5.   Advertise Without Paying a Penny

1.5.   Know your customers

For you to succeed in this business you need to understand your customers. To persuade someone or to motivate a client or to sell your service the key is to understand the person.

In my case my unique selling point was that I realised that there were a lot of people that wanted to rent cars but had no credit cards. They could not rent cars from the big rental companies.

That's the gap that I went on to fill. These customers with no credit cards can be found in any part of the world.

Now how do you service them? You ask for a cash deposit.

In order to understand your clients ask these questions:

- Who are they?
- Why do they want cars to rent?
- What language do they speak?
- Who else has offered them a similar car rental service?

Understanding these key questions allows you to draft a key unique selling proposition (USP) that others don't have.

The following are key Advertising Channels to use in the car rental business:

1.6.   Word of Mouth

This is the most effective selling method for the car rental business, especially when you have just started. Tell your friends, family members, workmates, classmates and anyone you have a conversation with.

Word spreads like wildfire. Once you do that, give that person a business card, tell them your car rental rates, the cars you have and tell him that you will appreciate his/her referrals.

By using this method alone you will have more business than you can handle in the first four months.

Don't overdo this especially if you don't have at least 5 cars because the business won't have capacity to handle more customer requests.

1.7.   Your own website for free

I created my first car rental business website in 30 minutes sipping coffee in a cafe and had it up and running at no costs. You can build your own professional website and have it look great without having to pay a professional designer or learn new code.

Here are three important takeaways you should remember when developing your site:

1. **Benefits:** Highlight clearly the benefits that customers will have by renting a car from you. These benefits should be unique that other companies charge a fee for, or those that they don't have. For example you can state benefits such as no credit card required, free car seats for babies, free GPS and maps for tourists etc., cheap rates etc. Put a lot of emphasis on the benefits that customers will have by renting from you, that way you are differentiating yourself from others.

2. **Audience:** Know your customers; this is probably the most important thing to do when designing your website content. Narrow down your message specifically for those customers. For example let's say your target market for your rental cars is tourists from South Korea who wants cars to rent. People from Korea don't drive manual cars, you highlight that you have automatic cars that cater for them. The other thing is that people from Korea have difficulties in understanding English thus you must provide a functionality that translates your website from English to Korean. Thus you design your website with your target audience in mind.

3. **Layout of your pages:** You should create a simple easy to navigate web page that's not cluttered. It should be easy to read. Here is a sample layout that you can use. It's got mainly these components: Home Page, Our Cars, Rates, Reservations, and Contact Us.

Exhibit 1 Sample Website Menu

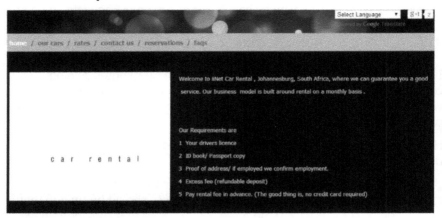

Exhibit 2 Contact Us

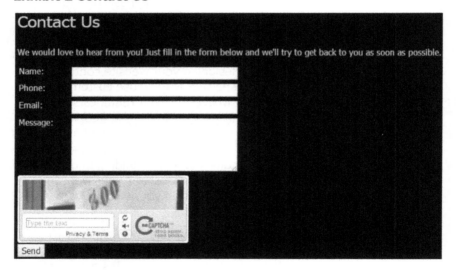

4. **Action:** It's critical that you highlight on your website what customers need to do for them to book cars right away. Highlight in big font or use buttons for words such as "Book Now" or "Contact Us". Don't design a site that leaves your clients guessing on what they need to do to reserve a car from you in advance.

5. **FAQs (Frequently asked questions):** These are self-explanatory; you need to provide answers to most of the commonly asked questions to your customers. Never leave your customers guessing for information. Here is a sample that you can use and some short answers

- Does car Rental B charge deposit? Yes you need to pay a deposit of R2600

- What are the requirements to rent a car? Copy of ID or passport, driver license and payslip

- How do I pay? You can pay by EFT or do a direct deposit into our bank account

- How many kms do I get per day? You get 200km free per day, excess kms attract a fee of R2.20 per km

- Can I cross the border with the car? No, the insurance does not cover crossing the border

- Are B Cars insured? All our cars are insured

- What happens if I get involved in an accident? The hirer is responsible for paying insurance excess, should the waiver be declined the hirer is responsible for the full value of the car.

More FAQS that you should provide answers to for your clients

- What happens if I get a traffic offence?

- How do I book a car or get a quotation?

- How do I cancel a booking?

- Are there any fees for modifying booking details or for cancelling a booking?

- Is a deposit required when I book?

- Will my card be charged at the time of booking?

- Can I pay with cash?

- Which cards do you accept for payment?

- Can someone else pay for my rental?

- Can I include an additional driver?

- Is there a young driver extra charge?

- Can I book for longer than a month?

- Do you lease vehicles?
- Is VAT included in the price?
- What type of driver's license is required?
- What is a Rental Agreement?
- What additional extras are on offer?
- How do I pay for the vehicle?
- What happens if I want to keep the vehicle longer than planned?

There are lots of free easy-to-use website builders on the internet, complete with drag & drop editors and an endless choice of templates and functions to help users like you create a website within minutes. Here are some of the recommended ones:

- **Wozaonline (www.wozaonline.co.za)**

This is an initiative to promote small businesses. The advantage of using them is that every website you create is well indexed by Google. This website is a Google initiative to promote small to medium enterprises (SMEs)

All you need is a Gmail account and the context of your services. Wozaonline offer the following for free:

- FREE easy-to-build professional website
- FREE sub-domain name on www.wozaonline.co.za
- FREE hosting
- FREE access to training materials and workshops

The major advantage of this online site is that once you create a website, you can track the number of visitors on your site and their location.

If a customer requests information on your site, you instantly get an sms and email notification all for free.

- **Wix (www.wix.com)**
- **Ucoz (http://www.ucoz.com/)**
- **Yola.com(www.yola.com)**

1.8. Post free online adverts

This is probably the most effective and free form of advertising method available today. You should take advantage of this as soon you start renting out cars. Don't overdo it especially when you are just starting because you will get flooded with clients and you won't have capacity to provide them the cars.

Here are the top advantages of the online advertising media:

1. It's free. Free classified ad sites will allow you to sell your car rental service without spending any money on advertising costs. Why pay to place an ad when there are ad sites that offer this service for nothing?

2. Its drives traffic to your site. With your car rental website, adding your web address to your classified ad will encourage customers to browse the other products that you are selling. A classified ad site is simply another place to put a link to your site, ultimately increasing your traffic.

3. It saves time. Most of us remember having to buy the newspaper to place an ad, then you must speak to someone in order to give them your details and often the ad will be removed after a week. Online classified ad sites only take a few minutes to join and submit your ad. You can also extend the duration of the ad online.

4. It is easy. Most online classified ad sites are easy to navigate, are browser friendly and are laid out in a clear and concise way. Truly, it is the easiest way to advertise hassle – free.

5. Easy result measurement. The fact that it's so easy to measure makes online advertising more appealing than the traditional advertising methods. You can find a lot of effective analytics tools in order to measure online advertising results, which helps you know what to do and what not to do in your following campaigns.

6. More targeted audiences. In comparison with traditional advertising, online advertising helps you to easily reach the targeted audience, which leads to your campaign's success.

7. Your potential sales are limitless. Selling your car rental services online in this way opens up a huge global market for your product. Local newspaper ads will only reach a certain number of readers and therefore a limited number of sales for you. There are over six million people online, many of which might be

looking for the exact product that you are offering. This makes placing a classified ad all the more appealing and has the potential to expand your business in a much shorter amount of time.

Samples of free classifieds that have made us money year after year.

Exhibit 3 Gumtree Advert

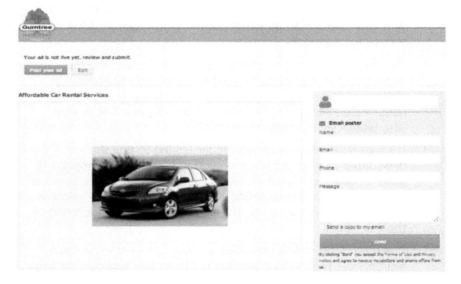

Date Listed: 2003-07-11

Location: South Africa

Welcome to B Car Rental, where we can guarantee you a good service. Our business model is built around monthly & Daily rentals

Our Requirements are

1. Your driver's licence
2. ID book/ Passport copy
3. Proof of address/ if employed we confirm employment.
4. Excess fee (refundable deposit)
5. Pay rental fee in advance. (**The good thing is, no credit card required)**

We have small economic cars that suit any traveller. We are here to save you money twice, on your rental and on your fuel.

Contacts us Today on +27 11 670 31888

Take advantages of some of free classifieds sites such as:

1. www.gumtree.co.za

2. www.vottle.com

3. www.olx.co.za

4. www.craiglist.org

5. www.junkmail.co.za

6. www.locanto.co.za

Begin by making a list of all free classifieds websites in your area.

1. Dos
In this step the key Dos to take note of are: • You want to make your advert highlight why you are more unique than big companies.   • Get a complete understanding of your prospect dos and don't, failing to do this is a waste of effort.
2. Don'ts
In this step the key Don'ts to take note of are: • Don't put adverts online without a pool of cars available. Those prospective clients will never come back again.

1.9. Direct Mail /Email Marketing

The beauty of using email is that it's an automated marketing channel. Here is how you do it. Sending marketing messages through email or email marketing is one of the most effective direct-marketing methods for car rentals especially when you are just starting. The advantage of this method is that it's relatively inexpensive to design, test, and send an email message. It also allows you to deliver messages around the clock, and to accurately measure responses.

Please be aware of the CPA regulations of email advertising, that you should have an option to unsubscribe or to reply Stop if any one of your recipients wishes to do so. Failure to do this violates consumers' rights.

How to do it.

Start by compiling a list of email addresses for the prospective clients that you have targeted.

Write a sales letter (advert). Start by introducing yourself and explaining in short summary the services you offer focusing on the cars that you have, different models of cars you offer, your daily, weekly and monthly rates.

Requirements

Here you detail in simple terms the things that clients will need to have to rent a car from you such as:

a) Copy of Identity Document

b) Copy of valid driver's licence

c) Proof of address

1. Dos
In this step the key Dos to take note of are: • In your email address refer to each customer by their name. This makes it more personal. • At the end of each email make sure you have your email signature. This will show your contact information such as your telephone and cell phone numbers, your website address, your email address as well as your physical address of the business. This is very crucial information for any prospective clients to have. They will always refer to you either on your website or call you in future should they require your service. It is an easy point of reference in future for those clients that might not need your services immediately but in future. • Provide information for the benefits of clients renting from you. Here you can explain other offers such as providing of GPSs and car seats.

1.10. Social Media (Facebook, twitter, Linkedin)

Social sites such as Facebook, Twitter and LinkedIn allow you to quickly notify your friends and family about your car rental services by the click of a button. I need not emphasise this, simply post a status update on your Facebook and tell them about the cars you have.

Here is a sample that I used and overnight friends and family were renting cars from me.

Exhibit 4 Facebook Advert that worked Magic

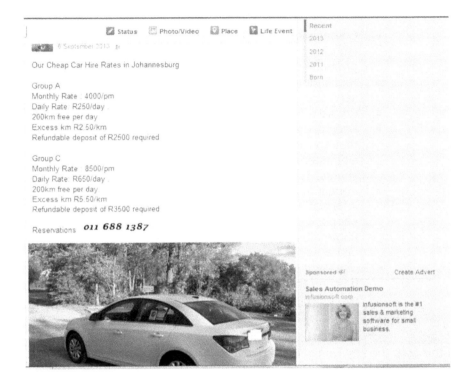

Status   Photo/Video   Place   Life Event

6 September 2013

Our Cheap Car Hire Rates in Johannesburg

Group A
Monthly Rate : 4000/pm
Daily Rate : R250/day
200km free per day
Excess km R2.50/km
Refundable deposit of R2500 required

Group C
Monthly Rate : 8500/pm
Daily Rate : R650/day
200km free per day
Excess km R5.50/km
Refundable deposit of R3500 required

Reservations   **011 688 1387**

Recent
2013
2012
2011
Born

Sponsored   Create Advert

Sales Automation Demo
infusionsoft.com

Infusionsoft is the #1
sales & marketing
software for small
business.

1. Dos

In this step the key Dos to take note of are:

- Communicate any latest news about your services e.g. launching new fleet or change of location or promotions.
- Highlight the benefits that customers get by using your services.
- Create a free Facebook page for your company.
- Keep it short and sweet. According to Facebook, posts that are on the shorter side — between 100 and 250 characters — get about 60% more likes, comments and shares. That's a big difference.
- Appeal to the visual sense. Not everyone processes information better through words. In fact, a lot of people learn by seeing, tapping their visual sense. Photo albums, pictures, and videos drive engagement on Facebook pages.
- Use Page Insights to help you learn. Page Insights is a function that allows you mine your analytics so that you can better reach out to customers.

2. Don'ts

In this step the key Don'ts to take note of are:

- Posting too often. The more often you post, the less the quality of your posts–or at least, that's the conclusion Facebook has come to. Because Facebook page rank concentrates on engagement of prior posts, posts with low engagement will actually hurt future page reach. So it's better to have one dynamite post, than many low-engagement posts.

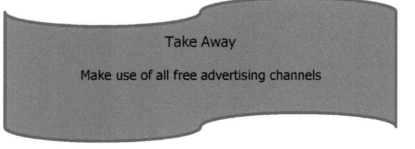

Take Away

Make use of all free advertising channels

6. What to do when prospective clients call in

"Successful people are always looking for opportunities to help others. Unsuccessful people are always asking, 'What's in it for me?'"

Brian Tracy

1.11. Get prospective customer details

With your advertising done and clients calling you looking for cars it's time to make sure that you get the right clients and eliminate the bad apples.

Prospective Client completes Business Form
Get the client to complete in full the following Renter Details Form shown in Exhibit 5 & 6. This business form contains all personal details of the renter such as first name, surname, home address, next of kin and work details.

Your Company Logo

Renter Details Form

Personal details

First Name: _____   Last Name: _____

Start Date: ___/___/___   ID #:..

End Date: ___/___/___

Email Address--

Address: _____

Suburb: _____   ....

Home Phone: _____   Mobile: _____

Next of Kin: _____

Relationship: _____

Address: _____

Suburb: _____   " _____

Home Phone: _____   Mobile: _____

Work details

Company Name: _____

Work Phone #: _____

Company Address _____

Exhibit 6: Renter Details Form

<Insert Business Name/ Company Logo>

Renter Details Form

First Name: _____ Last Name: _____

Date: _____ / _____ / _____

Position Title: _____

Gender: (circle one) M / F   Date of Birth:
_____ / _____ / _____

Address:
_____
_____

Suburb: _____   State: _____
Postcode: _____

Home Phone: _____   Mobile: _____
_____

Email Address:
_____
_____

ID # or Passport #: ▢▢▢▢ ▢▢▢▢ ▢▢▢▢

Details of Company & Next of Kin:

Company Name:
_____

Company Address:
_____
___

Company Phone Number:_____ Company email:-
_____

Next of Kin:
_____
_____

Relationship:
_____
_____

Address:
_____
_____

Suburb: _____   State: _____
Postcode: _____

Home Phone: _____   Mobile: _____
Work:_____

1.12. Verify customer details

During this step ask the customer for the following documents for verification purposes:
1. **Copy of drivers licence**
   You need to make sure the following things are in order:
   - Driver's licence is not expired.
   - Driver's licence is clear enough in terms of the person's picture.

2. **Copy of identity document or passport**
   - In case of passports check that it's not expired.
   - Check that the identity document is valid by looking up onto subscribed databases such as Searchworks or any other in your country.

3. **Copy of payslip**
Why do you need a copy of a payslip? This document allows one to get an idea of how much the client gets paid and see if they can afford to rent the car. It also empowers you to check and confirm with their employer that they genuinely work for that company. In this case you call their HR department and tell them that you want to confirm employment for one of their employees who wants to rent a car. They will gladly assist you in most cases.

Armed with these documents you need to check for the following things:
- Credit record check
- Criminal record

How?
In order to check a client's record you need to subscribe to companies that offer these services at a monthly fee. Examples of such companies in the context of South Africa are:
Searchworks
Lightstone

These subscription services give you information such as full personal information, address history, telephone history and employment history.

1.13. Type of clients you don't need to rent cars from you

As you get calls from prospective clients you will realise that your client base is huge, from training companies to movie makers etc. Be wise in your selection as to who you give the car to as some of these clients can cost you money.In this business it's critical that you get the right clients, here is the criteria of clients that will make you lose money.

- o People that are in a big debt: That's why it's important to check the client credit record and to see their payslip if they can afford to rent a car from you.

- o Those that have a criminal record : It's not a mistake or by chance that these people have a criminal record. You don't give them a rental car full stop. Giving them a car to rent is the fastest way to lose your car. Watch out for criminals.

- o Clients who have just had their car repossessed, their financial status and state of mind is questionable. You will have problems with them as they don't pay your rentals in time.

- o Companies that rent cars for shooting a movie: We once rented a car to a company that wanted a car for use in a movie. This is probably the worst decision you can make in a car rental business. We all know what happens in a movie, the car will be used for all sorts of things in the stunts. By the time our car was returned after a month it had depreciated by at least 60% in value.

1.14. Deny or accept rental application

Based on the outcomes of step 1 and step 2 you can either accept or deny a client application. This is done by notifying the client telephonically.

Dos
In this step the key Dos to take note of are: • Get all relevant documents before you give out the car. If the car gets stolen these documents are gold.
2. Don'ts
In this step the key Don'ts to take note of are: • Don't ever rent out a car to strangers without ever confirming and verifying their employer even if they have been referred to you by friends.

1.15. Signing Of Car Rental Contracts

Car rental contracts are the cornerstone of the business; they provide clients and businesses with a legal document stating the expectations of both parties and how negative situations will be resolved. The contract should be legally enforceable in a court of law and it's a tool to safeguard the company resources and prevent them from being abused by clients.

Exhibit 7: Long Term Car Rental Contract

Long Term Car Rental Contract **Terms and conditions** The below mentioned terms and conditions of the **Long Term Car Rental** shall bind the renter or additional renter whether he/she was driving the rented vehicle or not.
1. **Use of Vehicle**

1.1This Car Rental Agreement shall be entered into between the Company and any persons above the age of 18 years (or majority age in that specific country).

1.2The renter or any other listed and authorised person in this contract person(s) above the age of eighteen may drive this vehicle.

1.3The rented vehicle shall not be sublet to anyone.

1.4The rented vehicle shall not be used for any illegal activities.

2. Renter's Responsibilities

2.1Fuel

2.1.1The Renter is responsible for filling the fuel tank at the indicated level upon returning the car. Failure to fill the tank at the prescribed level will result in an additional charge to the Renter and the amount shall be deducted from his/her deposit.

2.2Keys
2.2.1The Renter is responsible for all lost car keys and / or a lockout situation.

2.3Damages
2.3.1The Renter is hereby responsible for all collision damage to the vehicle regardless if someone else is at fault or the cause is not known.

2.3.2The Car Renter is fully responsible for the cost of any repair up to the value of the vehicle.

2.4Traffic Fines and Other Penalties
2.4.1The Renter is responsible for the payment of all traffic fines or other fines, towing, any legal costs, or other violations, that the Car Renter may incur during the agreed Car Rental term period as indicated.

2.4.2The Renter is responsible for the full rented vehicle value that is not returned to the Car Rental Company.

2.5Insurance
2.5.1The Renter shall have his/her own Personal Insurance and Third party Insurance.

2.6Return of Rented Vehicle
2.6.1The Renter shall return the vehicle to the same location where the rented car was picked up for rental, on or before the agreed due back date and time.

2.6.2Additional fees will be charged for any overdue days if the vehicle is not returned as mentioned above.

2.7 Payment
2.7.1 The Renter is responsible for the payment of the rental fee and the deposit either by EFT, Cash Deposit or Credit Card.

2.7.2 **All payments are due on demand.**
Charges
Depending on the rented car (price range from R4 000 – R8 000 or even more per month plus deposit of R3 500) allocated kilometers' per month 2 000kms - 3 000kms and any excess fees will be charged per excess km.

3.	Termination of Contract

3.1Due notice either oral or in writing shall be given by either party prior to cancellation of the contract.

3.2Should the Company cancel the contract due the Renter being in breach, the Renter shall immediately return the vehicle, failure which the Company shall repossess the car whenever or wherever it is found and the Renter shall be liable for any costs incurred by the Company to recover the vehicle.

4.	Indemnity of the Company Renter

4.1The Renter agrees to indemnify the company and any of its directors, officers and employees for any loss of life damages or loss to property left or transported in the vehicle, or against any claim of any nature whatsoever and howsoever arising for any damage or loss which might be instituted against it.

5.	Mechanical Repairs and Accidents

5.1 The Renter shall advise the Company with immediate effect if the Renter has been involved in a car accident or when the vehicle has been damaged as a result of an accident.

5.2 The Renter shall advise the Company of any repairs that the vehicle requires and shall not undertake any repairs without the Company's consent.

5.3 Should the Company consent to the Renter repairing the vehicle due to it being an emergency or not to cause further harm to the vehicle, the Renter shall retain the invoices and submit them to the Company for compensation.

6.	Severability

6.1Except as expressly provided to the contrary herein, each paragraph, clause, term, and provision of this Car Rental Agreement, and any portion thereof, shall be considered severable. If for any reason, any provision of this Car Rental Agreement is held to be invalid, contrary to, or in conflict with any applicable present or future law or Regulation by any court in any proceeding between the parties, that ruling shall not impair the operation of, or have any effect upon, such other portions of this Car Rental Agreement as may remain otherwise intelligible, which shall continue to be given full force and effect and bind the parties hereto.

I the Renter and undersigned have read the terms and conditions and the annexed contract thoroughly and I fully understand it.

Signed by

Car Renter_____
         Date_____

Additional Car Renter_____
         Date_____

Company Representative_____
         Date_____

Exhibit 8: Short Term Car Rental Contract

Short Term Car Rental Contract
Terms and conditions
The below mentioned terms and conditions of the **Short Term Car Rental** shall bind the renter or additional renter whether he/she was driving the rented vehicle or not.

1.	Use of Vehicle

1.1This Car Rental Agreement shall be entered into between the Company and any persons above the age of 18 years (or majority age in that specific country).

1.2The renter or any other listed and authorised person in this contract person(s) above the age of eighteen may drive this vehicle.

1.3The rented vehicle shall not be sublet to anyone.

1.4The rented vehicle shall not be used for any illegal activities.

2. Renter's Responsibilities

2.1Fuel

2.1.1The Renter is responsible for filling the fuel tank at the indicated level upon returning the car. Failure to fill the tank at the prescribed level will result in an additional charge to the Renter and the amount shall be deducted from his/her deposit.

2.2Keys

2.2.1The Renter is responsible for all lost car keys and / or a lockout situation.

2.3Damages

2.3.1The Renter is hereby responsible for all collision damage to the vehicle regardless if someone else is at fault or the cause is not known.

2.3.2The Car Renter is fully responsible for the cost of any repair up to the value of the vehicle.

2.4Traffic Fines and Other Penalties

2.4.1The Renter is responsible for the payment of all traffic fines or other fines, towing, any legal costs, or other violations, that the Car Renter may incur during the agreed Car Rental term period as indicated.

2.4.2The Renter is responsible for the full rented vehicle value that is not returned to the Car Rental Company.

2.5Insurance

2.5.1The Renter shall have his/her own Personal Insurance and Third party Insurance.

2.6Return of Rented Vehicle

2.6.1The Renter shall return the vehicle to the same location where the rented car was picked up for rental, on or before the agreed due back date and time.

2.6.2Additional fees will be charged for any overdue days if the vehicle is not returned as mentioned above.

2.7 Payment

2.7.1 The Renter is responsible for the payment of the rental fee and the deposit either by EFT, Cash Deposit or Credit Card.

2.7.2 All payments are due on demand.

Charges

Depending on the rented car (price range from R400 – R800 or even more per day plus deposit of R2 500) allocated kilometers' per day 200kms - 300kms and any excess fees will be charged per excess km.

3.	Termination of Contract

3.1Due notice either oral or in writing shall be given by either party prior to cancellation of the contract.

3.2Should the Company cancel the contract due the Renter being in breach, the Renter shall immediately return the vehicle, failure which the Company shall repossess the car whenever or wherever it is found and the Renter shall be liable for any costs incurred by the Company to recover the vehicle.

4.	Indemnity of the Company Renter

4.1The Renter agrees to indemnify the company and any of its directors, officers and employees for any loss of life damages or loss to property left or transported in the vehicle, or against any claim of any nature whatsoever and howsoever arising for any damage or loss which might be instituted against it.

5.	Mechanical Repairs and Accidents

5.1 The Renter shall advise the Company with immediate effect if the Renter has been involved in a car accident or when the vehicle has been damaged as a result of an accident.

5.2 The Renter shall advise the Company of any repairs that the vehicle requires and shall not undertake any repairs without the Company's consent.

5.3 Should the Company consent to the Renter repairing the vehicle due to it being an emergency or not to cause further harm to the vehicle, the Renter shall retain the invoices and submit them to the Company for compensation.

6.	Severability

6.1Except as expressly provided to the contrary herein, each paragraph, clause, term, and provision of this Car Rental Agreement, and any portion thereof, shall be considered severable. If for any reason, any provision of this Car Rental Agreement is held to be invalid, contrary to, or in conflict with any applicable present or future law or Regulation by any court in any proceeding between the parties, that ruling shall not impair the operation of, or have any effect upon, such other portions of this Car Rental Agreement as may remain otherwise intelligible, which shall continue to be given full force and effect and bind the parties hereto.

I the Renter and undersigned have read the terms and conditions and the annexed contract thoroughly and I fully understand it.

Signed by

Car Renter_____
          Date_____

Additional Car Renter_____
          Date_____

Company Representative_____
          Date_____

41

Exhibit 9: Rent To Buy Agreement

Rent To Buy Sale Agreement

This is a Sale Agreement between

      Seller…………………………………………………ID#......................................
...

And

      Buyer…………………………………………………ID#......................................
...

: For the purchase of a Green Nissan Tiida (Car) with registration no. XXX XXXGP.

The purchase price of the car is R80 000, and the buyer paid a deposit of R30 000 on the ------of --------20XX, the balance of R50 000 which shall be payable in monthly instalments of a minimum of R3 000/pm. The balance shall attract an interest rate of 12% per annum.

The buyer acknowledges receipt of the car in its state and shall be responsible for all maintenance and servicing as well as other miscellaneous expenses/ and or costs like insurance, traffic fines (etc.)

The car is transferable from the seller to the buyer upon receipt of the last payment of instalments. The buyer will take insurance for the car.

In case of the buyer defaulting in his monthly instalments or other reasons arising from breach of the contract by the seller, the buyer has discretion to terminate this contract and request the buyer to return the car and for the seller to exercise further his discretion to deem fit the settlement of the matter.

Signed on this   day of   20XX

_____
Seller

Signed on this   day of   20XX

_____
Buyer

Signed on this   day of   20XX

_____
Witness

Dos

In this step the key Dos to take note of are:

- Make sure that there is a contract between you and the client; this is helpful as it is legally binding and all terms and conditions are in writing.
- In case any party is in default, the contract provides all the remedies to the problem.
- Make sure the client signs every page as this will show that he has read and acknowledged every page and details of the contract.
- Explain, or highlight some of the most important aspects of the contract: i.e. penalties, late returns and damage remedies should the car be damaged during the rental period.
- Make sure the FICA documents match details on the contract.
- Keep records of all contracts signed in case you might need them in future.

2. Don'ts

In this step the key Don'ts to take note of are:

- Never let a client take the car without signing the car rental contract.
- A checklist should also accompany the contract; this should never be left out. Remember to record any other consents that the client might have about the condition of the car, so that upon return there are no arguments.

Take Away

Make sure that the client is aware of any penalties in the contract

1.16. Car Rental Checklist

This checklist is a crucial part of the rental process when the client collects and returns the car.

Its sole purpose is to document the state of the car when the customer gets it. This includes any scratches, and dents on the car, if the car has a detachable radio, if a car seat or GPS was provided and the car mats etc.

Nobody works without a checklist, no matter how smart they are, from pilots to surgeons, even astronauts have a checklist. This shows you how important this is.

Exhibit 10 Car Rental Checklist

Car Rental Checklist

On Rental Checklist	Yes	No	Return Checklist	Yes	No.
Spare Wheel			Spare Wheel		
Spanner			Spanner		
Jack			Jack		
Jumpers			Jumpers		
Car Mats (How many)			Car Mats (How many)		
Car Radio			Car Radio		
GPS			GPS		
Other			Other		

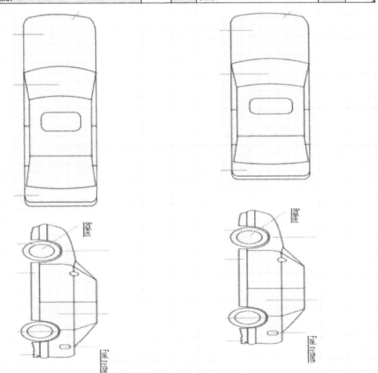

Client Name... Company Representative...

Client Signature.. Signature...

Key points to note:
a) Give the client a signed copy of the checklist and file your copy.
b) Remember the same checklist is the one that you will refer to when the client returns the car.
c) It is important to provide full tank of fuel in each rental car to clients and the clients shall return it with a full tank. Otherwise if the client does not return it full then applicable fuel monies will be deducted from their deposit.
d) Always record the mileage of the car before the client collects it.
e) Calculate mileage used on the car on its return by simply subtracting the current reading mileage and the initial recording when the car was collected. This will ensure that the renter does not exceed the allocated kilometers for that specific rental period.
f) Any excess mileage is charged for.

Example Mileage on collection 77 000kms
             Mileage on Return   78 000kms

Let's say your free kms = 300kms/day
And the car was rented for 3 days

Total free kms for 3 days = 300kms x 3 days =900kms
From the above recordings the client would have used 1,200kms

Therefore 1 200kms – 900kms = 300kms in excess.

Excess kms rate for example is R2.50

Total excess kms = 300kms * R2.50= R750

This means therefore that the client will have to pay an extra R750 on top of the rental fee paid.

It is very important that you explain to the client before they collect the car about the excess kilometers otherwise if the client is not aware of it, they will refuse to pay for it, thinking that it was included in the rental fee.

1.17. Payments

Dos
In this step the key Dos to take note of are: • All payments must be made upfront.   • Can have different types of payments, electronic funds transfer (eft), credit cards, and direct deposits.   • Deposits should also be made upfront together with the rental fee for the specific period.
2. Don'ts
In this step the key Don'ts to take note of are: • Never let the client take a car without payment or deposit because you will chase after your money which is time and resource consuming.

Exhibit 11   Car Rental Checklist

B Company Logo

TAX INVOICE

DATE:	
INVOICE #	
Customer ID	

B. Car Rental
Reg No: 20../0../0..
Address....

Tel:xxxxx xxxxxxx
email address
website address

BILL TO:
Client

Date	Description		Daily Rate
xx/xx/xxxx	Rental for Toyota corolla from xx/xx/xx- xx/xx/xx for x number of days at a Rate of RX/day		
		Total	R 0.00

Bank Details

7. Key Things to Know in Car Rental

1.18. Growing Your Fleet

In this chapter you will also learn through the processes provided to grow your fleet, that it is possible to start a car rental business with no car.

So how do you do this? It's simple, by using other people's cars! You might not have capital to start a car rental business but if you approach the right people with a good deal, you will be on your way to success of running a car rental business. Leverage is the key for this idea.

It is possible to start a business with no money at all, look at one of the largest, successful insurance company in this world, Federal Mutual. They started with no money but now they are the most well-known, big and successful insurance company.

"It's not money that's in the way of you starting your business. It's a mind-set."

John P. Hayes, co-author with Fred DeLuca, Subway's co-founder of *Start Small, Finish Big: Fifteen Key Lessons to Start-and Run-Your Own Successful Business*

By the end of the year, you should aim to have increased your fleet by three to four cars.

Here is how to do it:

Car Dealerships

In your local area or surrounding areas, find car dealerships and tell them about your business and how you wish to grow your fleet. There are car dealerships out there that are willing to sell you their cars in instalments whilst you are using it. You just have to agree on the instalment terms and you have got yourself a deal. Make sure that the car that you are buying from them is in good condition and does not give you problems; otherwise your deal will go sour.

If you meet your instalments and do not go in arrears, you will create a trust relationship with the dealership and you will always make deals with them. This will assist in growing your fleet.

Use other people's cars

This is another way of growing your fleet by using your parent's unused car, grandparent's car that has gathered up dust in the garage, your cousin's car, your friend or relatives.

The important aspect in this idea is that you make sure that you have a signed agreement and that you agree on all the terms and conditions of using their car in the car rental business. Make sure you inform them about the risks of the business as well as the long term benefits of it. Anyone would love your deal if you promise to keep extra income coming into their pockets. Make sure that this deal earns you money and that it does not cost you.

Agree on who will service the car, and how much they will be receiving for every rental. Once you have this in place you can do business.

Save, Save and Save.

This may seem impossible especially when you are starting, but remember this is a business of numbers, you must set your goals right at the beginning. Remember you are in this business to make money and the more cars you have the better. The trick in saving money is when you buy low cost maintenance cars, and the more clients you will definitely acquire. You will come to realise that each car will buy another car by the end of four to six months, if you play your cards right. Make sure that you charge right and that you have enough to survive on if you want extra income and enough to save to buy another car.

Rent to own from Sellers

You can rent to own a car from your relatives who are selling a car. Remember you are not buying your personal car, but a car to put in the car rental business. You can leverage with your clients as they will pay the car for you and at the same time you make some money.

Think of the house rental model, the landlord gets a bond from the bank but he does not live there but instead he puts tenants in the house. The tenants are paying his bond and at some point he will actually start pocketing some extra income for himself. Numbers, numbers, numbers,

I cannot emphasis this enough. Get it right the first time and you will make money.

Remember you are in it to win it. Make and get the best of every deal you make.

1.19. Maintaining You Fleet

It is vital that you maintain your fleet. The better condition your fleet is in the longer it stays and gives you more money. You don't want to have cars that constantly give you problems and take money out all the time. That is why it is important to buy the right cars; reliable, durable and low cost maintenance cars.

The list below will assist you in ensuring that you keep your fleet in good condition.

Service

Dos
In this step the key Dos to take note of are: • All tyres must be change or rotated periodically. • Service the cars according to the service kilometres. • Partner with a good, reputable car service garage or mechanic that will provide service for your cars every time you need them. • Keep records of all service information for all your cars. This will assist you in knowing which car and when service is needed.
2. Don'ts
In this step the key Don'ts to take note of are: • Don't wait until your car breaks down to service it as it is more costly. • Make sure that all clients that damage the cars pay for it so that you do not have to fork out money even when it is the client's fault, for instance clutch problems caused by the client.

Car Licence Disc

Dos
In this step the key Dos to take note of are: • Make sure your fleet has valid discs and always renew them every year. • Keep records of this so that you know when and which car needs a new disc. • Make sure that the right disc is on the right car. • Also check for those cars that were not registered in a certain province that upon registration of that car the licence number can change and therefore the number plates need to change accordingly.
2. Don'ts
In this step the key Don'ts to take note of are: • Never hire out a car without a valid licence disc as this is illegal and will attract a fine with the traffic department or your car can get impounded by police hence inconveniencing clients.

Insurance

It goes without say that motor liability risk and insurance costs are the biggest concern for a car rental business. It is important that you find the right car fleet insurance to protect your investment. Here is how my wife and I lost money by not renting out a car without insurance. We had recently traded in a car, with a client who had just purchased one of our cars that we wanted to dispose of. That same night we had a client enquire of a vehicle to rent. Very excited about having a client we decided to rent out the car.

At around midnight that very same night the renter called us and informed us that he was involved in a car accident. It was not the kind of news you expect to hear especially from a recently purchased car, we were left dumbfounded.

After taking the car to the mechanic, we were told that it was a write off. We were damned. We had just lost an investment we made in less than a day. The worst thing was that it had no insurance.

We were fortunate enough that the other party involved in the accident agreed to pay for the damages caused as she was in the wrong. We were paid for half the worth of the car. Well it was better than nothing. We also sold the damaged car to a car garage for sick money.

We ended up hearing from people we communicated with that the car renter was a drunkard, and we had made a huge mistake renting out a car to him.

1. Don'ts
In this step the key Don'ts to take note of are: <ul><li>Never hire out a car out to drunkards, if you see any signs of a bad client, don't ignore them. Go with your instinct and reject the rental application.</li><li>Take insurance for your fleet, don't wait a minute longer to do so, it might be too late.</li></ul>

Take Away

As your fleet grows have a car rental software that will assist you in taking reservations, tracks when a car needs to be returned, when a car needs to be serviced, when to renew car discs, when payments are due

Mistakes to Avoid

1. Never rent out your vehicle without insurance cover.

2. Ensure that your vehicle has a car tracker and other security systems for the safe keeping of your vehicle.

3. Never rent out a car to clients before verifying their details, this includes their residential address and employment details.

4. Always keep spare keys for each vehicle in case of key losses and other reasons.

5. Don't buy high maintenance cars especially if you are running on a low budget.

1.20. How to deal with problem Clients

Here is an interesting story of how a lady stole one of our cars. This is what happened: I had cars available and as usual my wife and I had put an online advert for prospective clients to see. Fortunately we had a client call responding to our advert enquiring about hiring the car for a long term period. We agreed to deliver the car to her at the address she provided us with. To be honest when we think about it now the signs were there but because she was a young lady who appeared so sincere we ignored it. She signed the contract for a 3 months long car rental and made payment in full of both the deposit and that current monthly rental fee and gave us her personal details, copies of driver's licence and identity document.

We were pleased indeed because a paying client is a good client. Little did we know that disaster awaited us?

As usual we send out invoices to clients as a reminder that payment would be due on a certain date for the car rental. She responded that she would make payment, fair and fine. However this did not happen. After her rental period expired a day later we sent another email and made several calls to her with regards to payment of the car rental but she insisted she would pay, until we realised that they were all stories. She even went to the extent of telling us that she had made payment, but from our side it never reflected in our account. Just so you know this is a sign for a bad client showing that they are freebie lovers, they would do and say anything to push their luck just to use your services for free.

After all those bogus stories we requested her to bring the car back as payment had not been made. This is when all hell broke loose. She was claiming that she was using up her deposit money now, and she even took the liberty of offering herself a daily rental fee which would suit her and prolong the use of the car. She now was in control on top of not meeting her payment obligations.

At this point we realised that she was not intending to bring the car back and that she was giving us an ultimatum. This is not good and besides we had every right to cancel the contract because she was in breach.

We decided to go collect our car, and to our amazement she did not reside at the place where we delivered the car anymore, she had moved. It turned out that she was going through a divorce and she had also quit her job and she was currently staying with a boyfriend. We were damned.

The thought of losing our investment just like that was daunting, and the worst thing of all was that the car did not have a tracker and it was going to be virtually impossible to track it down. Johannesburg is not a place to lose a car like that, theft is rife and that gave us the chills. We knew we were not going to find our car.

We went to the police to report our car stolen, but lo and behold the police told us that we had given away the car under an agreement, therefore the car was not stolen so we should find ways of retrieving it ourselves as they did not want to interfere.

We had to hire a private investigator to assist us in locating her or our car. At this point all we wanted was our car back. Sleepless nights took over our anxiety and worry during the day.

It became a costly adventure and eventually, the investigators managed to locate and find out where she would be at a certain time.

We took off and waited outside the specified premises around the time we were advised by the investigators. As we sat there we saw a similar car like ours passing by with two people inside, the driver being a man and a lady passenger but the strange thing was that the car had no number plates, apparently they had been removed. Fortunately we could identify it by some scratches and patches that it had. To our amazement the car did not enter the premises but it went to park at a shopping centre. Then a lady came walking pushing a stroller, but at that time we could not identify her, neither did it strike our minds that they actually had a plan in action.

It quickly dawned on us when we eventually identified her that, they did not want to go inside the premises in case someone noticed the car and perhaps someone would repossess it, and that the car that had parked at the shopping centre was our car. We did not even bother confronting her; all we wanted was our car. We were trying to avoid any unnecessary drama. We quickly drove to the shopping centre, with me holding the car papers so as to verify the car registration number on the car disc. I confronted the driver who at that moment had sensed something and had started the car engine ready to go. Fortunately I managed to stop him before he could take off.

The car attendants by the car park had started gathering and we told them that we were simply repossessing our stolen car. We emptied the boot which apparently was filled with clothes and we also found our number plates in the boot. The car was in the worst condition you can ever imagine. We left all of their belongings we found in the car in the parking lot and we drove away.

That was how we recovered and repossessed our car. I am sure you would agree with me that it was such a risky and dramatic event that no one would want to put themselves through. This is what happens if you do not plan your things well or take the right measures, to avoid this.

First and foremost it is important to make sure that you do your best in ensuring that you do not rent out your vehicle to people who have a potential of being problematic in future. However it goes without saying that as much as we might try to avoid bad clients, it is inevitable that sometimes we can have them, so how do you deal with them?

It's simple, just like when you cannot afford to pay for the bank's car, the bank repossesses it. The same concept is applied in the Car rental business to those clients that refuse to pay or are in breach due to any other reasons.

Repossessing your car is easy, if only you can locate it. Remember clients who refuse to pay are likely to have moved from where they stay or are no longer working where they used to work.

A tracker comes in handy at moments like these. The tracker company upon your request can locate your car and you can simply go and repossess it.

Always be cautious when repossessing cars from problematic clients. These clients can be in a desperate situation and can be violent. Always carry your car papers as proof that the car belongs to you. Also ensure that there are witnesses around to ensure that the client does not claim being assaulted and sue you.

This procedure can be very costly and time consuming especially if you do not have a tracker installed in your vehicle. The probability is that you might never recover your car.

1.21. Good Customer Service

In this business, keeping your clients happy is the key because this is how you retain them and get referrals. Know what your clients are looking for and provide exactly that. Remember word of mouth spreads like a wildfire and soon you will have clients flowing to you.

Before you know it you will not have capacity to service them, and that is why it is crucial to grow your fleet by exploiting some of the ways I have provided, if you want to grow your business.

So what is good customer service in a car rental business? Knowing what your clients need is fundamental to this aspect. You will meet clients who want you to deliver cars to them, pick up the car from their premises or the airport, clients who want you to drop them at the airport, all sorts of request. You have to be prepared for it and be happy to do so. You want to offer exceptional services so that your clients will remember you next time they are looking for a car to hire. Leave an unforgettable impression on your clients by the good service that you provide.

Remember, some of the requests from clients means more money. For instance dropping and picking up a car, attracts extra cost.

Growing means that you now have a good reputation with clients you serve and you are growing your own brand.

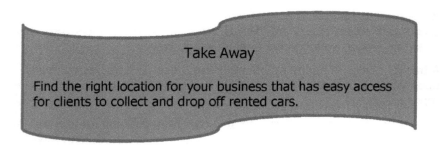

Take Away

Find the right location for your business that has easy access for clients to collect and drop off rented cars.

1.22. Legalities of running a car rental business

The Consumer Protection Act does affect a car rental business as you are in the business of service providing, therefore it is imperative that you keep abreast with these ever changing laws protecting consumers.

Important consumer rights to know in car rental.

- The consumer must be given a quote or breakdown of his/her financial obligations before entering into an agreement.
- The agreement a consumer enters into with a supplier must be in plain language that the consumer understands.
- No agreement must be longer than 24 months unless the consumer agrees to a longer period (in this instance, the supplier must prove that by extending the period, there is a financial benefit).
- A consumer must be allowed to cancel the agreement within 20 business days' notice.

- If cars rented are not suitable for their purpose, as communicated by the consumer to the supplier, the goods may be returned to the supplier.
- A booking or order of goods or services may be cancelled by a consumer.
- If services rendered are of poor quality, the consumer may request a refund of a portion of the purchase price from the supplier.
- If goods are defective, a consumer has 6 months from the date of delivery to return the goods to the supplier, at the supplier's risk and expense. At the consumer's choice, the supplier must fix the goods, replace the goods, or repay the consumer for the price paid for the goods (the voetstoots clause no longer applies).

8. Learn by Application

"The future depends on what you do today"
Mahatma Gandhi

Now that you know, take action. Have you ever wondered why movie stars such as Rambo, Bruce Lee and Walker Texas Ranger are so popular? These are men of action; nothing gets in their way to achieve their objective. For you to succeed in this business you have to be action driven.

Here are the key action basics to take every day in this business:

a) Tell everyone you meet about your business. Even if they won't rent your car, they will know who needs your services.
b) Get more cars, the money you make is directly related to the number of cars you have.
c) Make sure your cars are in good working condition all the time.
d) Provide extra services to your clients such as baby car seats and GPS for free.

Remember you can learn more by actually doing it and not just thinking about it. Take that first step to financial freedom and you will surely reap the benefits. Hard work will pave the way for your success in this business.

9.   Don't let fear and doubt hold you back

"The Man in the Arena"

"It is not the critic who counts; not the man who points out how the strong man stumbles, or where the doer of deeds could have done them better. The credit belongs to the man who is actually in the arena, whose face is marred by dust and sweat and blood; who strives valiantly; who errs, who comes short again and again, because there is no effort without error and shortcoming; but who does actually strive to do the deeds; who knows great enthusiasms, the great devotions; who spends himself in a worthy cause; who at the best knows in the end the triumph of high achievement, and who at the worst, if he fails, at least fails while daring greatly, so that his place shall never be with those cold and timid souls who neither know victory nor defeat."
Theodore Roosevelt

If these words don't rattle your cage then I don't know what else will. Get into business and start today. Fear and doubt are probably the two most crucial facts separating you from your dreams. I always ask myself what have I to lose anyway. Key factors to overcoming fear are knowledge and practice of courage. In order to eliminate fear, concentrate your thoughts on courage.

Take Away

Always remember not to allow Fear & Doubt to hold you back

10. Money Magnet

In conclusion it's important to note that you make money through service to others; that you get what you give, and for this reason you should consider it a great privilege to be able to give. One makes money by making friends, as you enlarge that circle of friends and being of great service to them and providing value, the more money you will attract. Be of great service to other people, by doing just that, the more money you make for others the more money you will attract to yourself. Here are the ten ways you can start applying today and make money in your car rental business:

1. **Start with small cheap cars.** Buy cheap small cars that are fuel efficient, cheap to service and easy to maintain. Save money for your customers. Buy cars cash from auctions. Buy cheap & maximise return on investment.

2. **Unique Selling Proposition (USP).** Let cheap be your USP and cater for the clients without credit cards. The customer should acknowledge anything special or unique about your rental agreement. Penalties must be clear to the customer. At the end of the day, it's your word against the customer's.

3. **Be obsessed with numbers.** It's critical that you know your numbers in an out; Critical numbers are your daily and monthly rental rates for your cars, free kms, rates per km for excess charges, insurance costs, tracker costs, service costs per every car in your fleet.

4. **Know your customers.** Identify exactly your target market and understand clearly what type of cars they need. That's key. If you are renting cars to Koreans for example they don't drive manual cars they only want automatic cars thus you cater for that market.

5. **When acquiring a vehicle, know when, where and how you're going to dispose of it.** Always have disposal plans for each and every car otherwise you will get stuck with liabilities.

6. **Manage risk.** Be selective as to who you rent your cars to, there are thieves out there, make sure your cars are insured and they have tracker fitted.

7. **Don't neglect sales and marketing.** Don't fool yourself that you are in the car rental business, you are in the sales and marketing business. Get this right and you will make money.

8. **Look for marketing partners.** If you've got hotels, lodges or car service companies propose a deal. Refer customers to them, and have them refer business to you. Put a brochure together that talks about your partnerships with the hotels, lodges, or put a phone in the hotel that dials your location. Be the rental car agency for the local convention centre.

9. **Move closer to your customers.** You want to move your business closer to where lot of people stay, for example closer to major airports, highways, shopping malls in these areas, that's where the money is.

10. **Rent to buy.** Get rid of old cars that are becoming too expensive to maintain by providing your loyal clients with a rent to buy option. Thus reducing your maintenance costs, insurance costs thus maximising your return on investment.

Take Away

Be of great service to others and money will follow you

11. Bonus Material

As part of this book I have included some free bonus Car Rental Business templates that you can start using right away. These templates are in word so that you can edit them to your liking and add your company name and logo. To get access visit and register on

www.startyourowncarrental.co.za.

WARNING

DO NOT READ THIS BOOK UNLESS YOU WANT TO START A CAR RENTAL BUSINESS WITH NO MONEY

Screw the banks and their money, start your car rental business today with one car and no loan. Whether you want extra income or make a million dollars, follow this step by step guide with everything you need to get started today, provided with all car rental templates.

In this step by step guide to starting a car rental business with no money.

You will learn:

- The car rental business model
- How to make money in car rental
- How to get started with nothing at all
- How to advertise without spending a penny
- Mistakes to avoid in car rental
- Dos and don'ts in car rental
- Ten ways to make money in car rental

Hey, whether you want extra income or you are a serial entrepreneur, this guideline book provides you with everything you need to get started today including:

- Car Rental contract templates
- Renter form details templates
- Car Rental checklist templates
- Car Rental Invoicing templates
- Sample marketing material
- Sample car rental sales letters

Lightning Source UK Ltd.
Milton Keynes UK
UKHW021835171218
334165UK00025B/1235/P